# CONTENTS

# ROUTE 1
## OVER THIRKLEBY WOLD

*This route over Thirkleby Wold takes you from the quiet village of Kirby Grindalythe over Thirkleby Wold via Cowlam to Sledmere. The village of Sledmere has many monuments worth exploring. Sledmere House, a fine Georgian house built in 1751 with gardens designed by Capability Brown, is open to the public. As is the Triton Inn but for a completely different reason!*

- - - o O o - - -

## FACT FILE
**Distance** - 18 miles (29km) or 21 miles (34km)
**Grading** - Moderate
**Off Road** - 50%
**Start Grid Ref** - Kirby Grindalythe
OS Landranger 101/905675
**Refreshments** - The Triton Inn, Sledmere

- - - o O o - - -

## THE ROUTE

Start from the village of Kirby Grindalythe. After leaving the West - Lutton road to enter the village take the first turning to the left, a dead end road. Bear right at the last house and enter the field on the left through a gate following the public bridleway sign.It is sometimes a rough ride along this bridleway, but it is signed with blue waymarks all the way, although some of them are a little faint. When the going gets tough keep roughly to the line of electric poles on the left. The track eventually bends right then left through a small waymarked gate, cross the field to a metal gate to join a farm track. Keep straight on here then where the track bends sharp right leave the track and go straight ahead through fields and after passing through more waymarked gates you arrive at West Lutton. At the road turn right along a long climb up to Thirkleby Wold. At a crossroad of bridleways turn left to pass the white triangulation Pillar on your left. After cresting the Wold the track joins a made up farm road for a good downhill bash to the main road.

Turn left at the road then at the crossroads turn right up the hill. In about 2 miles cross carefully over the busy B1253 to join the road to Cowlam. In half a mile turn left through the farmyard of Church Farm and follow the bridleway arrows round to the right then through a gate for a long downhill bash into a steep sided valley. You are now entering stock fields, take care! Once past the trees on the left the track opens out into a field. Bear to the right to find a waymarked small gate in the fence that descends from the right. Keep straight ahead now with the fence on the left to a signpost of bridleways. Turn right to follow the blue bridleway waymarks to the road. At the road turn left then in half a mile turn right along a wide chalk bridleway. In just over a mile at Sir Tatton Sykes Monument cross over the road to keep on the wide bridleway straight ahead. In a couple of miles turn right then right again at the main road into Sledmere. Take the second turn to the left on the Kirby Grindalythe road. In two miles you have a choice of routes.

You can either take the easy route back to Kirby Grindalythe and stay on the road or you can turn right along the bridleway to Squirrell Hall. This is a good bridleway which joins the one from West Lutton which you used earlier. Follow the bridleway arrows straight on at all times until you arrive at the crossroad of arrows that you met on the outward journey. This time go left (*almost straight on actually*) and return downhill to West Lutton village. At the main road turn left to take you back to Kirby Grindalythe.

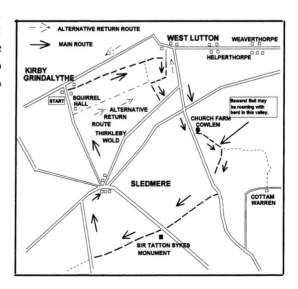

## ROUTE 2

## THE WETWANG WOBBLE

*A feature of Wetwang , apart from its odd sounding name, is the village pond. It is host to many unusual breeds of duck and boasts a resident pair of black swans. Alright, it is opposite the pub but I wrote this piece before sampling the superb ale!*

- - - o 0 o - - -

### FACT FILE
**Distance -** 12 miles (19km)
**Grading -** Moderate
**Off Road -** 60%
**Start Grid Ref -** Wetwang.
OS Landranger 106/934592
**Refreshments -** The Black Swan Inn, Wetwang
The Victoria, Wetwang

- - - o 0 o - - -

### The Route

Wetwang is situated on the A166 Driffield to Stamford Bridge road. Cycle in a westerly direction and shortly after leaving Wetwang turn left down the road to Huggate. At the first sharp corner leave the road and go straight ahead along a wide track signed as a public bridleway. At the bottom of the slope you will see a bridleway arrow on a post directing you left off the hedge onto a wide grassy track continuing straight ahead. In ½ mile turn left at the junction of bridleways. Then in another ½ mile just after a double bend look for an opening in the hedge on the right, there is a bridleway arrow on your left directing you through the hedge into the field. Follow the bridleway straight ahead along the field close to the hedge on the left. At the bottom of the field go right then where the hedge ends turn left onto a wider track to take you uphill to Angus Farm and eventually the road.

Turn right at the road then in a few hundred yards left at the bridleway sign. Keep on this wide track all the way to the valley bottom then turn left through a well signed gate. Keep straight ahead now for almost a mile and turn right at

6

the bridleway sign then eventually left to meet the B1248. Go left onto the road and pass through Tibthorpe village (*shop on left*), and continue up the hill. At the top near a bungalow on the right you will see a bridleway sign. Take this route and follow the blue arrows to exit onto a track. Turn right

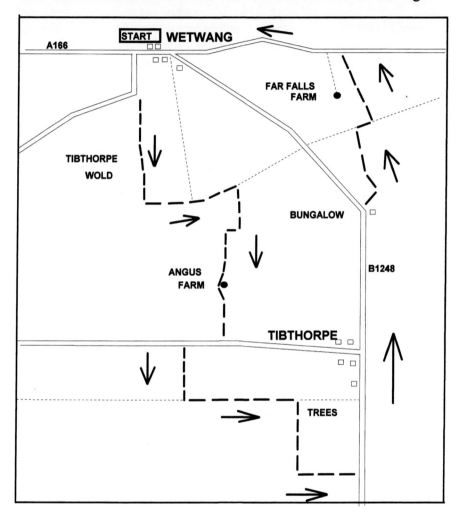

then immediately left onto another signed bridleway.This track takes you to the Driffield - Wetwang road in about a mile. Turn left here to return to Wetwang.

*I couldn't think of much more to say about this ride so I've drawn you a big route map!*

7

## ROUTE 3
## THE TIBTHORPE TIPPLE

*Perhaps it would be wise to ride this route after harvest as a considerable amount of the track is fieldside. Although there is plenty of room to ride it could be difficult in places with standing corn alongside the track. You do not need many instructions to find your way on this one it is quite straightforward. A long drag up, a hurtle down a quiet road then a long drag up again.*

- - - o O o - - -

### FACT FILE
**Distance** - 12 miles (19km)
**Grading** - Easy but tiring
**Off Road** - 60%
**Start Grid Ref** - Tibthorpe
OS Landranger 106/961555
**Refreshments** - The Old School Tea Rooms
and The Star Inn Hotel. Both at North Dalton

- - - o O o - - -

### The Route

Starting in Tibthorpe on the B1248 take the road south towards Bainton. Shortly the road goes uphill. Look out for the bridleway sign on your right where the trees start. Take this bridleway, it is fairly narrow and grassy but it soon opens out into a wider track. In about 1½ miles pass through a gate and keep straight on along a grassy valley to another gate. Straight on again here until in about 1 mile you exit onto the road to Haywold Farm. Keep straight on towards the farm following the bridleway sign until the road turns sharp right. Turn right with the road then go immediately left into a field track. Continue straight on for 1½ miles when the track goes sharp right then soon sharp left to enter a wide bridleway to take you to the road.

At the road go left and enjoy the run all the way to North Dalton, perhaps stopping for some refreshment. Turn left in the village then in a few yards where the road rises go left between the houses on a wide track, past the cricket field and picking up blue bridleway arrows all the way over the wold and down the other side to a gate into the wood. Follow the arrows through the wood and exit through a gate into a valley. This is the one you came on, this time turn right then in a few hundred yards at the hedge do not go through the gate. Instead, turn left up the hill and eventually onto a wide track to take you to the road. At the road turn right and hurtle along downhill most of the way back to Tibthorpe.

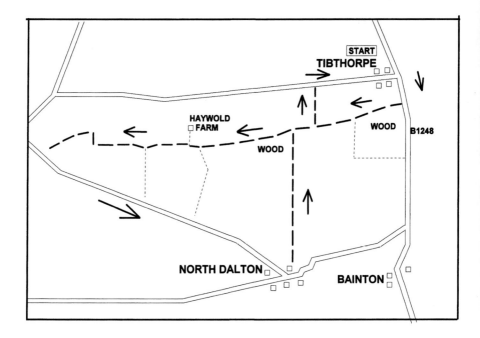

*This ride can be easily combined with route 2, the Wetwang Wobble to give masochists a longer tougher ride of over twenty miles. I will leave it up to you to devise which way you want to ride it!*

# ROUTE 4
## WALLOWING IN WARTER

*W*arter is situated in a most beautiful part of the Yorkshire Wolds. The village itself has some fine buildings, the thatched cottages dating from the early 1900's. They makes a picturesque setting for artists and photographers. Near the village are several springs of clear water and in 1132 it boasted an Augustine Priory. Of course the Romans showed their presence by building a station nearby called Delgovita.
We start the ride from nearby North Dalton another pretty Wolds village with its pond and church built on a mound. Please park carefully.

- - - o 0 o - - -

### FACT FILE
**Distance** - 15 miles (24km)
**Grading** - Easy
**Off Road** - 40%
**Start Grid Ref** - North Dalton
OS Landranger 106/935523
**Refreshments** - The Old School Tea Rooms
and The Star Inn Hotel. Both at North Dalton

- - - o 0 o - - -

## The Route
L eave North Dalton on the Huggate road in a north westerly direction then in 2½ miles turn left along the marked bridleway to Blanch Farm. Follow the bridleway signs through the farm then along well marked bridleways to eventually meet another bridleway coming in from the left. Take this bridleway, if you miss this junction of bridleways worry not as the bridleway you are on exits onto the same road.
At the road, regardless of how you arrived there, turn left to Warter. In the village turn right along the road towards Huggate then in 1½ miles keep right. One mile further on look out for a house on the right. Alongside the house is a signed bridleway to the right. Take this and follow the Minster Way to the road. Cross the road and continue along the wide bridleway still following the Minster Way, eventually crossing another road to follow the bridleway sign

10

opposite.In a short distance go right then left onto a bridleway to meet the farm road at Haywold Farm in about 1½ miles. Follow the farm road to the right and continue all the way to the road. You will see confirmation of the bridleway as you ride along. At the road turn left to return to North Dalton.

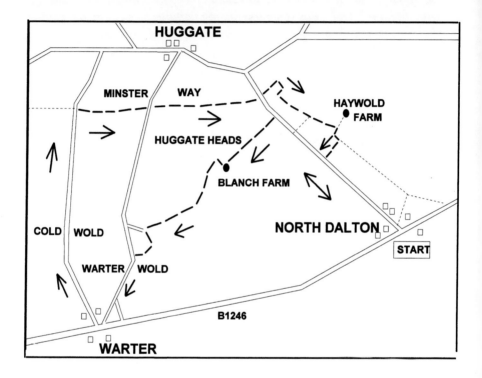

*Once again this route can be joined with earlier routes in the book to make a longer ride. Have a go at devising your own route using some of the bridleways suggested.*

# ROUTE 5

## THE GRIMSTON GRIND

*T*he deserted medieval village of Wharram Percy is near this route and is worth a visit if you take a short detour. The old church still stands, alas without a roof, and it has some interesting features as explained on site. For the non historical amongst you just turn those pedals to grind over the Wolds and enjoy the views.

- - - o 0 o - - -

**FACT FILE**
**Distance** - 14 miles (23km)
**Grading** - Easy
**Off Road** - 33%
**Start Grid Ref** - North Grimston
OS Landranger 100/843676
OS Landranger 101 for route detail
**Refreshments** - The Middleton Arms
North Grimston

- - - o 0 o - - -

## The Route

Start at the sign for bridleway and Centenary Way near the telephone kiosk at the bridge in the centre of the village. Cross the stream then turn left and further along the stream bear right under the old railway bridge. The route goes over parkland and through the right of two gates then bearing left and eventually onto a minor road. Turn left onto the road and enjoy the ride through pleasant farmland. Keep a wary eye out for the Bull! At the junction turn left to go to Wharram le Street. Go right at the crossroads then in about ½ mile right again towards Burdale and Fimber along a minor road.

In 1½ miles at a double bend turn right (*actually it is straight on as the road turns left*) along a farm road signed bridleway and Wolds Way. Keep on past the Tunnel Plantation, there is an old railway tunnel below ground here, and continue along the Wolds Way past North Plantation . When the Wolds Way goes left you must keep straight ahead onto a wider track which soon becomes a road. This takes you to a 'T' junction at Aldo Farm. Turn right here then right again at the main road to ride along to the pretty village of Birdsall. Pass through the village and bear right at the fork then just after the bends look out for the bridleway and Centenary Way sign in a wooded area on your right. Keep on this track until you meet the road then turn left. At the junction go right, then right again to return to North Grimston and the start.

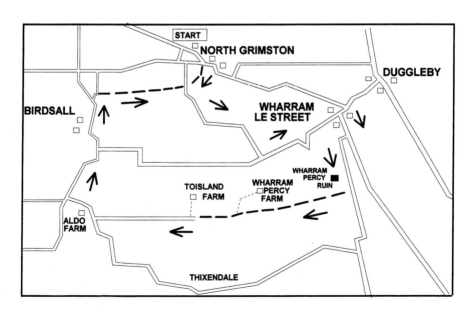

## ROUTE 6
## HUGGATE & THE MILLINGTON BULL

*Huggate is probably most famous for being cut off by the winter snows as it is one of the highest villages on the Wolds. The old village is built round a Well which is 350ft deep. The Roman looking large white gateposts with Latin inscriptions were supposedly built by Italian prisoners of war. Not as old as they look!*

*The route takes us near to Millington, a pretty village with an interesting small church. If a detour is made into the village you could take advantage of the cafe or pub for refreshment.*

*The Millington Bull? Oh yes I nearly forgot! When riding the section towards the Great Plantation the valley is often grazed by 'beasties'. Sometimes even a Bull, although usually docile if with its female friends. You have been warned!*

- - - o 0 o - - -

### FACT FILE
**Distance -** 18 miles (29km)
**Grading -** Moderate
**Off Road -** 40%
**Start Grid Ref -** Huggate
OS Landranger 106/882553
**Refreshments -** The Wolds Inn at Huggate.
The Cross Keys pub and
a restaurant at Fridaythorpe.
The Ramblers Rest Tea Rooms and The Gate inn
at Millington. (*If detour taken*)

- - - o 0 o - - -

### The Route
Turn into the village at the junction almost adjacent to the Wolds Inn. Follow the road until it becomes a track to take the bridleway of the Wolds Way straight ahead. It is a fieldside ride eventually falling into Horsedale following the bridleway north into Holm Dale eventually exiting onto a wide track. Go straight ahead here continuing along to Fridaythorpe, you might wish to visit the Cross Keys!

14

Leave Fridaythorpe on the A166 towards Stamford Bridge and continue along for 4½ miles. Almost opposite the radio mast at the top of Garrowby Hill turn left across Bishop Wilton Wold to Great Givendale. At Great Givendale, where there is a road leading right into the village centre, look left and turn along a bridleway on the left signed as the Minster Way. Follow this all the way to the road. Turn left here then in 1½ miles turn right along the bridleway farm road which soon becomes a track over a field. It is a good downhill bash now that becomes steeper and steeper but be warned, it ends at a fence so make sure your brakes are in good working order! At the road turn left along Millington Dale, a quiet country road. In 1¼ miles look out for a bridleway sign on the left directing you through a gate along a grassy valley. You might encounter livestock with the possibility of a Bull roaming with the herd. If you do not wish to venture into the unknown simply continue along the road and go straight on at the junction to return to Huggate. For those of you with a taste for adventure enter the valley and ride along to the Great Plantation at the end, climbing

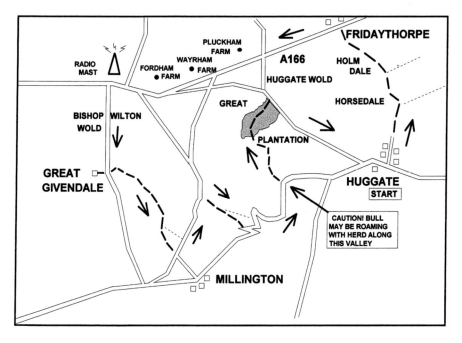

uphill to exit onto a narrow road. Turn right at the road and in about 2 miles go left at the junction to return to Huggate.

## ROUTE 7
## TRACKING OVER MOWTHORPE WOLD

*K*irby Grindalythe is a quiet village nestling in the valley between Thirkleby and Mowthorpe Wolds. There is only limited street parking here so if there is any difficulty you could park at Sledmere and pick up the route from there.

- - - o 0 o - - -

### FACT FILE
**Distance** - 21 miles (33km)
**Grading** - Moderate
**Off Road** - 40%
**Start Grid Ref** - Kirby Grindalythe
OS Landranger 101/905676
**Refreshments** - The Triton Inn at Sledmere
The Three Tuns at West Lutton

- - - o 0 o - - -

### The Route

Kirby Grindalythe is situated on the road which runs between Duggleby on the B1253 and Foxholes on the B1249. Leave the village in a northerly direction and turn left at the 'T' junction towards Duggleby. Immediately look to the right for a bridleway sign through a gate into a field. Cross the field into another field through the gate ahead. Straight on now climbing all the time and in ½ mile you will see a small gate and bridleway signs on the left. Follow the bridleway to the left through the gate to join a white road to some trees. Soon the road bends to the left through the trees then right now keeping the trees on your right. Follow this track which becomes a tarmac farm road keeping straight ahead at all times. Eventually sweeping to the left and downhill onto the road.

Turn left at the road then in about ½ mile at the farm on the right follow the bridleway sign down to the buildings. Take care here as there is a lot of farm machine activity as well as large lorries. There are some faded bridleway arrows to guide you but you might not see them so I will guide you through. Turn right on the wide concrete road past the large buildings on the right and

16

carefully go straight ahead between this and other buildings. Keeping straight on will bring you to a wide, white road. Follow this bridleway over the wold to the road in 1½ miles. Go left at the road taking the B1253 into Sledmere. Turn right at the junction then in about ½ mile turn left along a quiet road signed to Wetwang. In a little over 2 miles as you are sweeping downhill be prepared to brake just past the cottages on the left to take the signed bridleway to the left to Sir Tatton Sykes monument.

Left at the monument onto the road to Sledmere. In Sledmere take the third turning to the right to Kirby Grindalythe. It is a long pull as you climb onto Thirkleby Wold and at the top in about 1½ miles turn right at the bridleway sign for Squirrel Hall. Follow the blue bridleway arrows past the Hall and

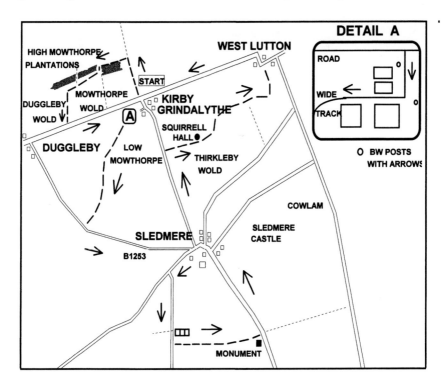

through the wood eventually arriving at a crossroad of bridleways. Keep left here (*almost straight on*) and blast downhill to West Lutton. Turn left at the road and cycle carefully back to Kirby Grindalythe.

*If time allows have a look round Sledmere to see the monuments, the Well and some of the ornate architecture on the estate houses.*

17

## ROUTE 8
## WOBBLING AROUND WINTRINGHAM

*A* *variation of terrain on this ride from fieldside track to wide Wolds bri dleways. There is also a variety of livestock to be negotiated! You will find beasts in fields across Mowthorpe Wold with the possibility of a Bull roaming with the herd. The bridleway over Linton Wold is a good track, unfortunately it passes Rayslack House where there are guard dogs so be careful and don't pat them on the head!*

- - - o O o - - -

### FACT FILE
**Distance** - 15 miles (24km)
**Grading** - Moderate
**Off Road** - 40%
**Start Grid Ref** - Wintringham
OS Landranger 101/884731
OS Landranger 100 for route details
**Refreshments** - Out of luck this time!

- - - o O o - - -

### The Route
Wintringham is signed off the A64 between Scarborough and Malton. The route starts on a bridleway at the A64 end of the village opposite Thorndale Farm along the Wolds Way. Carefully follow the waymarks across the narrow bridge, (*the brave might like to ride through the beck*) and through the gate and across the middle of the field diagonally right to a small gate in the hedge opposite. Keep following the obvious track at the side of the field past a small covered reservoir to meet a narrow road. Cross the road and take the bridleway opposite then follow the waymarks, don't miss the one through the gap in the hedge on the right half way along, and after a few gates you will reach the village of Thorpe Bassett.

Turn left and meander through the village and along a narrow, quiet road which climbs over Thorpe Bassett Wold to a 'T' junction in 1½ miles. Turn left here and cycle along this country road for 3½ miles. Be careful not to miss the bridleway at a kink in the road opposite the sign for Rayslack House. Turn right along the fieldside track at the bridleway sign and continue all the way following waymarks to exit onto the road at Kirby Grindalythe. You may have had some 'wee beasties' to contend with! Left at the road for 1½ miles then just past Thirkleby Manor Farm look for the bridleway along a wide

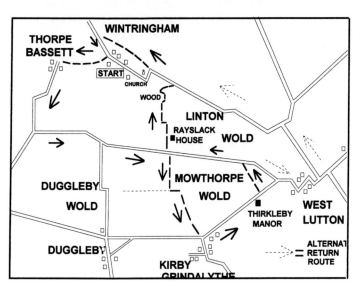

track on the left which takes you to join the road in ½ mile. Go left and cycle for 1½ miles to the bridleways at the entrance to Rayslack House and this time take the route past the house keeping a careful eye

out for the dogs. (*This is a superb bridleway but if you don't like the idea of passing Rayslack House turn right at the exit of the last bridleway and go to West Lutton. After the double bends in the village turn left then keep to the left to Wintringham.*) Once past the house and buildings follow the waymarks over Linton Wold across fieldside tracks, through a wood to finish with a flurry on a wide downhill track. Be careful along this loose surface as a good turn of speed can be built up and it is easy to misjudge the surface and fall off.

For those of you who stayed in the saddle and weren't savaged by the dogs turn left at the road towards Wintringham. As you enter the village at the first corner turn right onto a wide bridleway, signed as a bridleway and the Wolds Way. In ½ mile turn left at the road to return to Wintringham village.

## ROUTE 9

## THE BOYNTON BASH

*B*oynton is a pleasant village on the B1253 out of Bridlington not far from the historic village of Rudston famous for its monolith. The views from the Roman Road are fantastic across to the sea in the east and an all round vista of the Wolds and their pretty villages nestling in the hollows. This route is not much of a Mountain Bike ride although there are some good bridleways included. Just enjoy it for the scenery, I did!

- - - o 0 o - - -

### FACT FILE
**Distance** - 14 miles (22km)
**Grading** - Easy
**Off Road** - 25%
**Start Grid Ref** - Boynton
OS Landranger 101/136680
**Refreshments** - The Bosville Arms at Rudston
The Star Inn & The Bay Horse at Kilham
Try the ice-cream at the Post Office in Kilham!

- - - o 0 o - - -

### The Route

Turn off the B1253 at Boynton following the sign for 'Boynton village south only'. Park on the roadside here with respect for others and cycle back towards the B1253. Turn left and ride to Rudston. On the left entering the village is the church with the huge Monolith protruding from the ground. Some say the stone was thrown by the Devil to destroy the church but he missed! Others think that is has some Pagan significance - can't you just feel the atmosphere? No? Ok then ride through the village as far as the Bosville Arms then turn left for Kilham. Oy! That means you sneaking into the pub! Keep on the road for Kilham, go left at the junction near the cemetry then at the 'T' junction in the village go left towards Bridlington. At the first sharp right hand bend go straight on *(in theory its a left turn)*. This is the Roman Road called Woldgate and climbs high onto the Wolds. At the junction go straight ahead then in a few yards leave this road and turn right continuing

20

along the Roman Road. In about half a mile turn left at the bridleway sign. Keep a sharp eye out for the sign as it is hidden by the hedge from this direction.

It is a pleasant ride along the bridleway, quite wide if a little bumpy. It climbs then falls down to a junction of bridleways. Turn right here and follow the waymarks across fields and eventually into some trees with a hedge on the left. At the end of the trees go through the gap in the hedge then continue straight ahead with the hedge now on your right. You will see a confirmation bridleway sign along the way and you will soon reach the road.

At the road go left and at the crossroads turn right. In about 1 mile at a line of trees turn left along a wide bridleway between the trees. At the road turn right then in a few yards go left at the bridleway sign across a field. There are two stiles to lift your bike over but I am sure this will not be a problem. Over the second stile go straight ahead through the nettles and down a short, steep bank to exit onto the farm road. Go left at first then right around the building on the right turning left over the bridge in a few yards. Follow the wide path straight ahead and you will return to the start at Boynton village south.

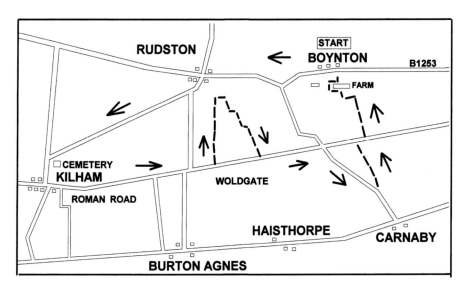

## ROUTE 10
## THE FRIDAYTHORPE FROLIC

*The route uses one or two bridleways of earlier routes but introduces some new and interesting tracks to make this circular tour of the central Wolds area an attractive ride. There are plenty of pubs en-route for your enjoyment, not that I am saying you should sample the brew at each one! But on a hot summers day.........!!*

- - - o 0 o - - -

## FACT FILE
**Distance** - 17½ miles (28km)
**Grading** - Moderate
**Off Road** - 60%
**Start Grid Ref** - Fridaythorpe
OS Landranger 106/875590
**Refreshments** - The Cross Keys pub and a restaurant
in Fridaythorpe. The Wolds Inn at Huggate.
The Black Swan at Wetwang

- - - o 0 o - - -

## The Route

Fridaythorpe, situated on the busy A166 is not the prettiest village on the Wolds but perhaps one of the most convenient being placed between York and Driffield. It boasts a pub, a restaurant and a mostly Norman church. Our route follows the Wolds Way at the start which is along a narrow lane near the telephone kiosk. It is signed as the Wolds Way and bridleway. Follow the lane until it becomes a wide track for a few hundred yards. Where the wide track goes left you must go straight ahead where you will see the Wolds Way sign and bridleway. Follow the signs along Holmedale leading to Horsedale turning left eventually onto a fieldside track which joins the farm road a little further along. Keep on this track until almost at Huggate ignoring the Wolds Way sign to the right to continue into Huggate village along a narrow lane.
At the road 'T' junction turn left past *(or into)* the Wolds Inn then follow this

quiet road almost to Wetwang, keeping left at the two junctions. Half a mile before the A166 at a right angle left bend in the road look out for the bridleway sign on your right. If you reach the main road you've missed it and must retrace your steps. Follow the bridleway arrows to a junction of bridleways. Go left here on a grassy hedge lined track all the way to the B1248 without deviation. Cross the road with care and continue straight ahead along another bridleway. The track soon narrows but keep straight on and shortly look diligently for a bridleway sign in the hedge on the left. Take this fieldside track to reach the A166. The next bridleway is almost straight across towards the farm at Garton Field. Follow the signs leaving the farm track and continue straight

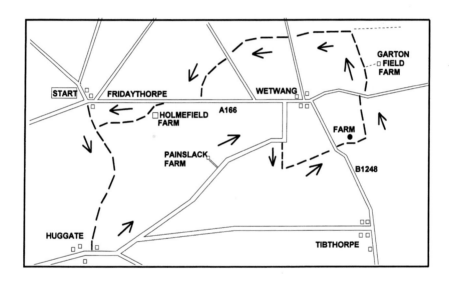

ahead along a fieldside track to join a wide grassy bridleway in about ½ mile. Turn left along this track, keep straight on crossing over two roads still following the wide bridleway to eventually reach the A166. (*If you wish to visit the pub in Wetwang turn left at the first road then return to this point after your refreshment*). Turn right at the A166 and take care on this busy road. In about a mile look for a bridleway sign on the left along a wide farm road. This 'green lane' climbs steadily to meet the wide track from Fridaythorpe which you used at the start. Keep on the wide track all the way to return to Fridaythorpe village.

# TRAILBLAZER BOOKS

## CYCLING BOOKS
Mountain Biking around the Yorkshire Dales
Mountain Biking the Easy Way
Mountain Biking in North Yorkshire
Mountain Biking on the Yorkshire Wolds
Mountain Biking for Pleasure
Mountain Biking in the Lake District
Mountain Biking around Ryedale, Wydale & the North York Moors
Exploring Ryedale, Moor & Wold by Bicycle
Beadle's Bash - 100 mile challenge route for Mountain Bikers

## WALKING BOOKS
Walking into History on the Dinosaur Coast
Walking around the Howardian Hills
Walking in Heartbeat Country
Walking the Riggs & Ridges of the North York Moors
Short Walks around the Yorkshire Coast
Walking on the Yorkshire Coast
Walking to Abbeys, Castles & Churches
Walking around the North York Moors
Walking around Scarborough, Whitby & Filey
Walking to Crosses on the North York Moors
Walks from the Harbour
Walking in Dalby, the Great Yorkshire Forest
Walking in the Footsteps Captain Cook
Ten Scenic Walks around Rosedale, Farndale & Hutton le Hole
Twelve Scenic Walks from the North Yorkshire Moors Railway
Twelve Scenic Walks around the Yorkshire Dales
Twelve Scenic Walks around Ryedale, Pickering & Helmsley

## DOING IT YOURSELF SERIES
Make & Publish Your Own Books

## THE EXPLORER SERIES
Exploring Ryedale, Moor & Wold by Bicycle

## YORKSHIRE BOOKS
Curious Goings on in Yorkshire
The Trailblazer Guide to Crosses & Stones on the North York Moors

**For more information please visit our web site:**
**www.trailblazerbooks.co.uk**